Block Island

ONE OF THE LAST GREAT PLACES

Photographs of Block Island by **Gerard P. Closset**

Foreword by **Neil Lang**

Gerard P. Closset

Block Island

"I enjoy traveling and recording far-away places and people with my camera. But I also find it wonderfully rewarding to see what I can discover outside my own window. You only need to study the scene with the eyes of a photographer". - Alfred Eisenstaedt

First Printing, 2012 ISBN 978-1-4675-2694-4

Library of Congress Control Number: 2012937394

Front Cover: Old Harbor with the National and Surf Hotels in the Background

Credits

All photos in this book by Gerard Closset

Cover and interior design by Kristen Kiley

Created, produced and designed in the United States. Printed by Friesens in Canada

Dedication

This book is dedicated to all those who love Block Island...

And to my beloved wife Nicki for her consistent, loving support, to my jewel of a daughter, Juliette and special son-in-law Jeff, and in loving memory of my younger daughter Jennifer, who loved my photographs and believed so much in my talent... She inspired me to develop a website, show my work in galleries and wanted me to create this book. I miss her terribly.

Foreword

To be asked to write about the creator of any form of art is a challenge. However, when the artist is a close friend, the challenge becomes more overwhelming. All the same, I have accepted this challenge with pleasure and honor, for I not only greatly admire Gerard Closset's work, but also take pride in knowing him for almost forty years.

This presentation of his photographs so well reflects its description as "One of the Last Great Places in the Western Hemisphere" as it was designated by the Nature Conservancy a few years ago.

Gerard has hiked and biked endlessly and observed the trails that crisscross the island from the high cliffs and bluffs on the southern side to the sandy stretches of beach on the east, to the northern tip and its iconic "North Light", and down along the coves and rocky beaches of the west side. His subjects range from the myriad of stonewalls that define older farmlands and land parcels and the broadness and sparseness of the windswept terrain.

We are made aware of places he has discovered and visited– perhaps many times before, but each time with a new meaning... Each time perhaps delving deeper – a relationship, an observation made in layers over time.

The work concentrates on a particular aspect of the subject and place. Those individual forms of nature – the ocean, the land, the sky, the stonewalls - that are observed and explored at different seasons and at different times – make us understand and comprehend the whole. One is made aware of the sensitive clarity in his capture of the brilliant whiteness of a winter day and the multi-colored palette of an autumn field. A red gate through a stonewall in a snowstorm, fog-shrouded stonewalls and the singularly placed red cedar trees that stands alone. A stonewall corner and a church beyond on a winter's afternoon. The details and gracefulness of the Victorian and New England architecture. The broadness of the landscape as well as the minuteness of a flower petal or a grasshopper on a leaf.

This portfolio is a personal diary, set in no particular time. In this photographic essay he offers not only these captured images, but the expression of the feelings and inner response that were evoked as he became involved in their selection...

A glimpse of Block Island emitted from his vision and his response to it. Enjoy the view...

Neil Lang / Artist
Block Island, RI, January 2012

Introduction BLOCK ISLAND THROUGH THE EYES OF GERARD CLOSSET

The title of this book refers to the Nature Conservancy's designation of Block Island as "One of the 12 last great places in the Western Hemisphere". Ever since my first visit many years ago I have known this little speck of an island to be a very special place. This feeling only grew with time and was later confirmed by the Conservancy's accolade. Ever since this first visit, capturing the natural beauty and special nature of the island through the imagery of my photography has been a very personal quest, a quest that became more exciting as my knowledge and experience as a photographer grew. For over 30 years I have been passionate about taking pictures of Nature and Wildlife and have traveled around the world to destinations off the beaten path seeking photo opportunities. Yet Block Island remains my favorite place, a place where I am connected through my photography and friends, a beautiful and relaxing haven, a throwback to a simpler time when life was slower paced.

Located near the Rhode Island coastline, Block Island is home to year-round and seasonal residents as well as a summer destination for thousands of visitors seeking beautiful beaches and harbors. The island however has so much more to offer to those who venture beyond the beaches, shops and inns of Old Harbor. Its inland scenery is one of great, subtle beauty, the soul of the island that evokes a bygone era. This has only been made possible by the Block Islanders' wonderful effort to preserve the character of the island, resulting in a remarkable amount of land (over 40%) in conservancy. This is an achievement I attribute to an unusually strong sense of community and stewardship. I also truly hope that my photography, in a small way, contributes to the preservation effort by showing what could be lost... The lands in conservancy are accessible to the public through an extensive system of hiking trails, a privilege I often take advantage of. When I set off on the "Greenway" and "Clayhead" nature trails lugging my camera equipment, I am rewarded with views of fresh ponds, wetlands, green-rolling hills traversed by stonewalls, old farms, 19th century lighthouses and other landmarks, tranquil meadows and striking panoramas that encompass coastal bluffs, sand dunes and the ocean. I have discovered these walks to be a wonderful way to commune with nature and a powerful inspiration for the images I record. Every year I try to find new ways to capture the island's essence and uniqueness and year after year I discover new perspectives even in places I know well.

All images in this book are of Block Island. I have tried to capture its essence and its mood in different ways. Every season has its own special pull on me, particularly when the bustle of summer is replaced by the serenity of a relaxed and colorful fall, a magical season on Block Island. The colors change to pastels and brilliant yellows and reds in ways so different from the mainland, and the island takes a different, more subdued character that invites reflection. The oft-present Block Island fog transforms everyday landscapes into wonderful, mysterious, ghostly, vanishing scenes that pull on this photographer, a mood I tried to capture in several images. As every photographer has discovered, the light of early morning and late afternoon can turn familiar places and objects into incredibly special and vibrant scenes, as with pictures of fishing boats in Old Harbor at sunrise or Sachem Pond and the Sullivan House at dusk. Autumn leads into the cold winds, nor'easters and long, gray stormy days of winter. All seasons evoke different feelings and moods, and all provide wonderful photo opportunities in this one "Last Great Place".

All images in this book can be purchased as prints or showcase products from my website (www.exoticwildlifephotos.com) or by contacting me at: clossgpc@mac.com.

Previous page, Block Island Ferry Entering Old Harbor (Aerial). Above, Fishing Boats and *Carol Jean* in Old Harbor.

Fishing Boats in Old Harbor.

Previous Page, Fishing Boats and Fog at Sunrise
at Old Harbor. Right, Hotel Manisses Cupola.

Left, Statue of Rebecca, "Goddess of Temperance" on Block Island. Right, the Surf Hotel. Next Page: View from the Surf Porch.

Previous Page, Southeast Light at Sunset. This Page,
Harbor Church in the Snow.

Mitchell Farm. Next Page, Leaning Old Barn near Dunn's Cartway.

Path to Crescent Beach in the Fall.

Previous Page, Fisherman and the Block Island Ferry. Fishing Boats at Old Harbor. Overleaf, Fall on the Westside.

Stonewall and Trees in the
Fog. Next Page, Red Gate in
Nor'easter Snowstorm.

Previous Page, Southeast Light in the Fog. Above, Full Moon over the Southeast Light.

Toy Sailboats in the Window. Next Page, Sailboat by the Coast Guard Station at Sunset.

Block Island Farmer's Market.

Page 31, Sunset at Dorrie's Cove. Previous page, Surf at Pebbly Beach. Above, Blue Dory Inn.

The Gothic Inn. Next Page, the Spring House Cottage. Overleaf, the Spring House Hotel.

Previous Page, the Spring House Annex. Above, Windswept Cottage.

Red House. Next Page, Figurehad Building and Storefront on Water Street.

Previous Page, Beach Stone Art near the North
Light. Right, Path to the North Light.

Previous Page, Sachem Pond and the North Light at Dusk. Above, the North Light.

Sachem Pond in Winter. Next Page, Driftwood on Grace's Cove after a Storm.

Dunn's Cottage. Next Page, Cottage on Dunn's Cartway.

Previous Page, Block Island Stone Wall. Above, Greenway Hiking Trail. Overleaf, the West Side Baptist Church.

Blue Gate and Barn.

Grasshopper on Hydrangea. Next Page, White Water Lily in Pond across the Painted Rock.

Dune Roses and Fence by the Beach. Right, Boats in Old Harbor at Sunrise. Next page, Sullivan House at Sunset.

Previous Page, Sunset on Great Salt Pond from the Sullivan House. Above, Sunset near Dorrie's Cove. Next Page, Black Rock Cove.

One of Yesterday's Beloved Ferries, the *Yankee*.

Block Island Cemetery in
Snow Storm.

Old Harbor in Morning Fog. Next Page, Tree and Stonewall in the Fog.

Previous Page, Black Rock Bluffs. Above, Fourth of July Parade. Overleaf, Adirondack Chairs and Sunset on the Westside.